Praise for ...

the furious longing of God

"Sometimes I think that Brennan Manning's books should come with tear marks and nicotine stains. He dares to write who he is, and in so-doing never fails to shape and change me into a more human, more honest disciple. *The Furious Longing of God* is one of the most startling apologetics for hope you will read this year."

Pete Greig, one of the founding leaders
of The 24-7 Prayer Movement

the ragamuffin gospel

"In our society, we tend to swear unyielding allegiance to a rigid position, confusing that action with finding an authentic connection to a life-giving Spirit. We miss the gospel of Christ: the good news that, although the holy and all-powerful God knows we are dust, He still stoops to breathe into us the breath of life—to bring to our wounds the balm of acceptance and love. No other author has articulated this message more simply or beautifully than Brennan Manning."

Rich Mullins, songwriter and recording artist

"I found deep comfort in realizing that Jesus loves even me, a ragamuffin, just as I am and not as I should be; that He accepts me, though I am most unacceptable. I came to this book hungry; I tasted and saw afresh that our God truly is good and that He is, after all, for us."

Michael Card, musician, recording artist, and author of *A Violent Grace*

"So much religion is conveyed to us as bad news or bland news that we are immensely grateful when it is spoken freshly as good news. This is a zestful and accurate portrayal that tells us unmistakably that the gospel is good, dazzlingly good."

Eugene Peterson, author of *The Message*

"Brennan Manning does a masterful job of blowing the dust off of shop-worn theology and allowing God's grace to do what only God's grace can do—amaze."

Max Lucado, bestselling author of *No Wonder They Call Him the Savior* and *God Came Near*

"Some books are a great read. Some have taught me lifelong lessons that have made my life more of what I'm sure God intended it to be. And of course some have impressed my friends but gathered dust on my shelves. *The Ragamuffin Gospel* was and is different. It transformed me. I will never be the same."

Michael W. Smith, Michael W. Smith Productions

abba's child

"Brennan is my friend, walking ahead of me on the path toward home. As I watch him from behind, I am drawn to more closely follow on the path, to more deeply enjoy Abba's love."

Dr. Larry Crabb, author of *Inside Out* and *Finding God*

"Brennan awakens a sense of wonder at the possibility of real relationship with the Abba of Jesus. I was gently led closer to becoming a true child of Abba."

Michael Card, singer, songwriter, and author of
Immanuel: Reflections On the Life of Christ

"Brennan Manning has the wonderful gift of making Jesus a real answer to our real questions, a desirable lover for our ever desirous hearts. He does it again in *Abba's Child*."

Richard Rohr, founder of the New Jerusalem Community in Cincinnati and the Center for Action & Contemplation in Albuquerque the furious longing of God

brennan manning

the furious longing of God

foreword by mark batterson
afterword by claudia mair burney

David C Cook®

transforming lives together

THE FURIOUS LONGING OF GOD
Published by David C Cook
4050 Lee Vance View
Colorado Springs, CO 80918 U.S.A.

David C Cook Distribution Canada
55 Woodslee Avenue, Paris, Ontario, Canada N3L 3E5

David C Cook U.K., Kingsway Communications
Eastbourne, East Sussex BN23 6NT, England

The graphic circle C logo is a registered trademark of David C Cook.

The Web site addresses recommended throughout this book are offered as a
resource to you. These Web sites are not intended in any way to be or imply an
endorsement on the part of David C Cook, nor do we vouch for their content.

Unless otherwise noted, Scripture quotations are the author's own translation.

LCCN 2008942916
Hardcover ISBN 978-1-4347-6750-9
International Trade Paperback ISBN 978-1-4347-6728-8
eISBN 978-1-4347-0086-5

Published in association with the literary agency of Alive Communications, Inc,
7680 Goddard St., Suite 200, Colorado Springs, CO 80920

The Team: John Blase, Amy Kiechlin, and Jaci Schneider
Cover Design: The DesignWorks Group, Charles Brock
Cover Images: Clouds © age fotostock/SuperStock;
other images are Shuttershock

Printed in the United States of America
First Edition 2009

9 10 11 12

111315

contents

foreword

by Mark Batterson

lead pastor of National Community Church and

author of *In the Pit with a Lion on a Snowy Day*

If Brennan Manning writes it, I'm going to read it. It's as simple as that. I've been greatly impacted by his previous books, especially *The Ragamuffin Gospel* and *The Importance of Being Foolish*. So when I was given the opportunity to write the foreword to this book, I was truly humbled. And I selfishly accepted because it meant I would get to read the book before you!

Brennan has a raw poetic writing style that puts him in rare writing company. His words will gracefully confront the status quo in your life and reawaken a deep desire to know the One who desires you. Brennan also has a way of putting into words the subliminal fears and hopes and desires many of us have a difficult time verbalizing. That's why his books resonate with readers on such a deep level.

It was C. S. Lewis who said, "We need to be reminded more than instructed." And that's what this book was for me, a timely and timeless reminder of what's most important. Simply put, the furious longing of God for each and every one of us.

To say that Brennan Manning has blazed new trails in this book would not be true. He has not. But to say that Brennan Manning is attempting once more to plow up the hardened ground of our hearts, now that would be a true statement. And he has, at least for me.

Brennan writes as a man knee-deep in his Abba's love. And his words convey more than information to the mind. They are revelation to the spirit. Every Christian knows that God loves him or her. Unfortunately, that fact often remains a tenet or tenant of the mind. And until it gets into your heart, it remains information. Once it gets into your heart, it results in transformation. I believe this book will help translate information into transformation.

As I read *The Furious Longing of God,* I was struck, once again, by Brennan's profound grasp of God's grace. Somehow he's able to turn the kaleidoscope and reveal new patterns of truth that I'd never noticed before. And the simple reminder he offers is exactly what I needed to know: *The Father not only loves you, but likes you.*

As you read these pages, I hope you don't just hear Brennan's voice. I hope you hear the heart of your heavenly Father. He furiously longs for you!

a word about *consider this*

Each chapter concludes with a couple of questions and thoughts worth considering. Whether you come up with some "right" answer is not the goal. The hope is that they will cause you to pause and spend just a little more time with the themes of the chapter.

Remember, the Father desires to say something to *you* in these pages. Such is His furious affection for *you*. Such is His love for *you*.

intro

I'm Brennan. I'm an alcoholic.

How I got there, why I left there, why I went back, is the
story of my life.

But it is not the whole story.

I'm Brennan. I'm a Catholic.

How I got there, why I left there, why I went back, is also the
story of my life.

But it is not the whole story.

I'm Brennan. I was a priest, but am no longer a priest. I was a
married man but am no longer a married man.

How I got to those places, why I left those places, is the story
    of my life too.
But it is not the whole story.

I'm Brennan. I'm a sinner, saved by grace.
That is the larger and more important story.
Only God, in His fury, knows the whole of it.

For two years, between 1971 and 1973, I lived with a community
of Franciscans in Bayou La Batre, Alabama. Three were priests,
two were lay brothers. I was thirty-five years old at the time, the
adventure of my faith in full sail. The shore was a port city, the second largest in the United States, after the one in New York.

A few of us worked on the shrimp boats there whenever
they needed help. It was short-term work, ten days at sea,

trawling for shrimp, flounder, snapper. We were always careful when we went to sea. Always.

One day we were on our way home from Beaumont when we caught the end of a Texas tailstorm. The water was calm at first. And our forty-five-foot-long boat bobbed lazily in the water like the boat on the cover of this book. But suddenly the clouds gathered and the temperature dropped. The sea began to churn, sweeping spray across the bow. Waves pummeled the sides of the boat. Our seasoned captain told us to get below. Below deck, we reached for metal handles and dear life.

I was convinced we were going to die.

Then the storm, the real storm, hit. Winds of 120 miles per hour. Sudden swells ten feet high. It was a fury unleashed.

Someone once said, *If a man would learn to pray, let him go to sea.*

My life has been a life lived in God's furious longing. And I have learned to pray.

genesis

The genesis of this book originated in 1978 during a thirty-day silent, directed retreat at a spiritual center in Wernersville, Pennsylvania. My director, a Jesuit priest named Bob Hamm, guided me to a passage in the Song of Solomon:

> I AM MY BELOVED'S,
> AND HIS DESIRE IS FOR ME.
> (7:10 NASB)

This is the passage I prayed for the duration of my time there.

Over the past thirty years, I have prayed that passage (Song of Solomon 7:10ff.) in soaring 747s, monasteries, caves, retreat centers, and deserted places. I believe His desire for you and me can best be described as a *furious longing*. If you don't get anything else out of this book, I hope you begin to pray that passage. When you take those words personally, I mean very personally, a number of beautiful things come to pass:

- The drumbeats of doom in your head will be replaced by a song in your heart, which could lead to a twinkle in your eye.
- You will not be dependent on the company of others to ease your loneliness, for He is Emmanuel—God with us.
- The praise of others will not send your spirit soaring, nor will their criticism plunge you into the pit. Their rejection may make you sick, but it will not be a sickness unto death.
- In a significant interior development, you will move from I *should* pray to I *must* pray.
- You will live with an awareness that the Father not only loves you, but likes you.

- You will stop comparing yourself with others. In the same way, you will not trumpet your own importance, boast about your victories in the vineyard, or feel superior to anyone.
- You will read Zephaniah 3:17–18 and see God dancing for joy because of you (the *Jerusalem Bible* translation is accurate).
- Off and on throughout the day, you will just know that you are being seen by Jesus with a gaze of infinite tenderness.

I am a witness to these truths.

There is no need to mince words. I believe that Christianity happens when men and women experience the reckless, raging confidence that comes from knowing the God of Jesus Christ. I've said that before in books and talks, and it'd be blasphemous for that not to show up here at the beginning of this book.

In my forty-four years of ministry, the furious love of God has been the dominant theme of my life. I've varied with titles such as *Ragamuffin Gospel*, *Abba's Child*, and *The Relentless Tenderness of Jesus*, but they are all facets of the same gem: that the shattering truth of the transcendent God seeking intimacy with us is not well served by gauzy sentimentality, schmaltz, or a naked appeal to emotion, but rather in the boiling bouillabaisse of shock bordering on disbelief, wonder akin to incredulity, and affectionate awe tinged by doubt.

The furious longing of God is beyond our wildest desires, our hope or hopelessness, our rectitude or wickedness, neither cornered by sweet talk nor gentle persuasion. The furious longing of God, as Dan Berrigan writes, is "not to be reduced to a thing, a grand ideal; it is not to be reduced to a plaything, a caged songbird, for the amusement of children." It cannot be tamed, boxed, captivated, housebroken, or templebroken. It is simply and startlingly Jesus, the effulgence of the Father's love.

The seldom-stated truth is that many of us have a longing for God and an aversion to God. Some of us seek Him and flee Him at the same time. We may scrupulously observe the Ten Commandments and rarely miss church on a Sunday morning, but a love affair with Jesus is just not our cup of tea.

I don't really think that about you. If that were the case, you wouldn't have searched the couch cushions for change to buy this book. I am writing *The Furious Longing of God* truthfully and candidly, to share of the God who has revealed Himself in my personal history. After you've read it, I hope you'll drop it at a used bookstore where some ragamuffin will pick it up and she'll say, "Cool." Then maybe she'll pass it on to some poor wretch who is bedraggled, beat up, and burned out, and he'll shout, "Wow!"

I am witness to the truth that Abba still whispers:

COME THEN, MY BELOVED,
MY LOVELY ONE, COME.

FOR SEE, WINTER IS PAST,
THE RAINS ARE OVER AND GONE.

FLOWERS ARE APPEARING ON THE EARTH.
THE SEASON OF GLAD SONGS HAS COME,

THE COOING OF THE TURTLEDOVE
IS HEARD IN OUR LAND.

THE FIG TREE IS FORMING ITS FIRST FIGS
AND THE BLOSSOMING VINES GIVE OUT
THEIR FRAGRANCE.

COME THEN, MY BELOVED,
MY LOVELY ONE, COME.
(SONG 2:10–13 NJB)

CONSIDER THIS...

1. When you read that phrase—the furious longing of God—what emotions or images does it evoke?

2. "... I *should* pray to I *must* pray." How would you describe the difference between the two?

fury

The noun *fury* is commonly associated with extreme anger. However, when the *Oxford Dictionary of Current English* discusses "the fury of a gathering storm," the meaning morphs into intense energy.

When one of England's finest writers, G. K. Chesterton, spoke of "the furious love of God," he was referencing the enormous vitality and strength of the God of Jesus seeking union with us.

Another ragamuffin, Rich Mullins, sought to describe the same longing of God:

> *In the reckless raging fury*
> *that they call the love of God.*[1]

I miss my good friend.

Employing adjectives such as *furious, passionate, vehement,* and *aching* to describe the longing of God are my mumbling and fumbling to express the Inexpressible. Yet, I plod on. Both theology, which is faith seeking understanding, and spirituality, which is the faith-experience of what we understand intellectually, offer a glimpse into the mystery. Now we see only reflections in a mirror, mere riddles (1 Cor. 13:12). But someday, the adjectives will give way to the reality.

But then there's also that word Chesterton used: *union.* That's one of the most explosive words in my Christian vocabulary. The daring metaphor of Jesus as bridegroom suggests that the living God seeks more than an intimate relationship with us. The reckless, raging fury of Yahweh culminates, dare we say it, in a symbiotic fusion, a union so substantive that the apostle Paul would write:

IT IS NO LONGER I WHO LIVE,
BUT CHRIST LIVES IN ME.
(GAL. 2:20 NASB)

In a fascinating footnote to that verse, the *Jerusalem Bible* adds: "The living acts of a Christian become somehow the acts of Christ." (Gulp!)

My critics, and there are and have been many, protest that I write too much about the love of God and not enough about sin and judgment and hell and how to keep Christ in Christmas. They claim that I am unbalanced, unsound, and a little bit crazy. While I plead guilty to that last charge, I am confident that God will raise up other unbalanced, unsound, and crazy writers to cry with me the French Easter liturgy:

L'amour de Dieu est folie!
L'amour de Dieu est folie!
(The love of God is folly!)

Elsewhere I've written that Jesus came not only for those who skip morning meditations, but also for real sinners, thieves, adulterers, and terrorists, for those caught up in squalid choices and failed dreams.

> I HAVE COME TO CALL NOT
> THE SELF-RIGHTEOUS, BUT SINNERS.
> (MATT. 9:13)

This is a passage to be read and reread because every generation has tried to dim the blinding brightness of its implications. Those of us scarred by sin are called to closeness with Him around the banquet table. The kingdom of God is not a subdivision for the self-righteous or for those who lay claim to private visions of doubtful authenticity and boast they possess the state secret of their salvation. No, as Eugene Kennedy notes, "it is for a larger, homelier, and less self-conscious people who know they are sinners because they have experienced the yaw and pitch of moral struggle." The men and women who are truly filled with light are those who have gazed deeply into the darkness of their own imperfect existence.

For twenty-one years, I tried desperately to become Mother Teresa. I lived around the world in griming poverty and depersonalizing squalor. I lived voluntarily for six months in the garbage dump in Juarez, Mexico—garbage there as high as your ceilings. It was a place filled with everyone from four- and five-year-old children to senior citizens in their eighties, all crawling over broken whiskey bottles and dead animals, just to find something to eat or possibly sell to hawkers on the side of the road. I've lived voluntarily as a prisoner in a Swiss prison; the warden there believed priests shouldn't be chaplains but actual prisoners. Only the warden knew my identity. I've lived on the streets of New York City with eleven-, twelve-, and thirteen-year-old prostitutes, both boys and girls, and ministered to them through Covenant House. I just knew if I could become a replica of Mother Teresa, then God would love me.

Pretty impressive, right? Yeah, right.

That's just a part of who I am. The rest of Brennan Manning is a bundle of paradoxes and contradictions. I believe in God with all my heart. And in a given day when I see a nine-year-old girl raped and murdered by a sex maniac or a four-year-old boy slaughtered by a drunken driver, I wonder if God even exists. As I've said before, I address Him and I get discouraged.

I love and I hate. I feel better about feeling good. I feel guilty if I don't feel guilty. I'm wide open, I'm locked in. I'm trusting and suspicious. I'm honest and I still play games. Aristotle said I'm a rational animal. But I'm not. That's some of the rest of Brennan.

Ironically it was April Fool's Day, 1975, 6:30 a.m., and I woke up in a doorway on Commercial Boulevard in Fort Lauderdale, Florida. I was thick in an alcoholic fog, sniffing vomit all over my sweater, staring down at my bare feet. I didn't know a wino would steal my shoes during the night to buy a bottle of Thunderbird, but one did. I had been out on the street for a year and a half, drunk every day, sleeping on the beach until the cops chased me away. You could find me in doorways or under the bridge, always clutching my precious little bottle of Tequila. And it wasn't just that this good Franciscan priest drank too much. I broke every one of the Ten Commandments six times Tuesday: adultery, countless acts of fornication, violence to support my addiction, character assassination to anybody who dared to criticize me or remonstrate with me.

The morning I woke up in the alcoholic boozy fog, I looked down the street to see a woman coming toward me, maybe twenty-five years old, blonde, and attractive. She had her son in hand, maybe four years old. The boy broke loose from his mother's grip, ran to the doorway, and stared down at me. His mother rushed in behind him, tucked her hand over his eyes, and said, "Don't look at that filth. That's nothing but pure filth." Then I felt her shoe. She broke two of my ribs with that kick.

That filth was Brennan Manning, thirty-two years ago. And the God I've come to know by sheer grace, the Jesus I met in the grounds of my own self, has furiously loved me regardless of my state—grace or disgrace. And why? For His love is never, never, never based on our performance, never conditioned by our moods—of elation or depression. The furious love of God knows no shadow of alteration or change. It is reliable. And always tender.

So I am proud only of those days that
we pass in undivided tenderness.
—Robert Bly

My experience of His furious love often fills me with a fury as well when I hear well-known preachers and televangelists distorting Abba's image. Jesus says, "Live in me. Make your home in me just as I do in you" (John 15:4 MSG). *Home* is a place of welcoming love, nonjudgmental acceptance, accompanied by many signs of affection. His invitation to intimacy is startling, contrary to all the pontifications of certain religious leaders and champions of deuteronomic morality. Their unbending rule-keeping petrifies His furious compassion. This should not be so.

The awesome love of our invisible God has become both visible and audible in Jesus Christ, the glory of the only Son filled with enduring love. The apostle Paul prays for us all in Ephesians 3:17–19 (NASB):

> THAT YOU, BEING ROOTED AND GROUNDED IN LOVE, MAY BE ABLE TO COMPREHEND WITH ALL THE SAINTS WHAT IS THE BREADTH AND LENGTH AND HEIGHT AND DEPTH, AND TO KNOW THE LOVE OF CHRIST WHICH SURPASSES KNOWLEDGE, THAT YOU MAY BE FILLED UP TO ALL THE FULLNESS OF GOD.

Do you hear what Paul is saying? The love of Christ is beyond knowledge. We've got to let go of our impoverished, circumcised, traditionalist, legalistic, human perceptions of God and open ourselves to the God in Jesus Christ. If we will, the promise is that we will be filled up with the fullness of God. That is truly good news!

So much of what was presented to me as real in bygone days, I now see as fictitious. The splenetic god of alternating moods, the prejudiced god partial to Catholics, the irritated god disgusted with believers, the warrior god of the "just" war, the fickle god of casuistic morality, tut-tutting our little weaknesses, the pedantic god of the spiritually sophisticated, the myriad of gods who imprisoned me in the house of fear; I could go on.

Von Balthasar's credo rings true to me: "Love alone is credible." The real God of unrestricted love corresponds to the Jesus of my journey.

The closer I come to death, the less inclined I am to limit the wisdom and infinity of God. The confession of John the apostle that *God is love* is the fundamental meaning of the holy and adorable Trinity. Put bluntly, God is sheer Being-in-Love and *there was never a time when God was not love.* The foundation of the furious longing of God is the Father who is the originating Lover, the Son who is the full self-expression of that Love, and the Spirit who is the original and inexhaustible activity of that Love, drawing the created universe into itself.

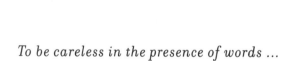

To be careless in the presence of words ...
is to violate a fundamental morality.
—N. Scott Momaday

It is always beneficial to acknowledge that books can be deceptive. The most lyrical prose on the furious longing of God creates the illusion that we have already arrived at beatitude. Then after reading a paragraph or so, you have to return to the sheer ordinariness of your life, to days that bring the same thing over and over again, the drudgery of routine; as the Buddhists say, "the laundry." Rather than being appalled by the discontinuity between the poetic and interesting and the prosaic and mundane, it serves well to fasten on the utter delight of a loving God who is deeply touched that, in the brouhaha of your busy life, you would devote even five minutes to spiritual reading.

A similar and more sophisticated snare entices the writer. After a scintillating sentence such as "You belong to the quivering coterie of the debauched languishing in exile" or some such breathtaking words on "the coruscating beauty of the living God," the writer discovers with alarm that his prose has made him artificial and insincere. Slavish attention to precise and proper words can seduce the author into a certain kind of posturing with the catastrophic result that he or she loses touch with his or her broken humanity. The danger of elegant accomplishment besets every artist. What to do? All I have learned through trial and error is to stay alert and aware, especially of God smiling at our silliness.

CONSIDER THIS...

1. There is the "you" that people see and then there is the "rest of you." Take some time and craft a picture of the "rest of you." This could be a drawing, in words, even a song. Just remember that the chances are good it will be full of paradox and contradictions.

2. On page 37, I listed some fictitious gods presented to me in the past: the splenetic god, the prejudiced god, the irritated god. Come up with at least one more, from your history, to help round out the list.

our Father

I'd like to draw your attention to one of those deeply moving passages in chapter 11 of Luke's gospel. It is one that has had a profound impact on my personal life. In the scene, Jesus appears to be exhausted with ministry; He's had it up to here with people and He wants to be alone, so He steals away from the crowd to find a quiet place to pray. In a very short time, the disciples notice His absence and set out in pursuit. As they pass through the Kidron Valley, they almost stumble over Jesus. He's on the ground, mute, motionless, utterly absorbed in prayer. They had never seen a man pray before as Jesus prayed. They wanted to pray as Jesus prayed.

So when at last He arose from the ground, one of the disciples said, *Lord, teach us to pray.* It was in the words that followed

that Jesus of Nazareth revealed to women and men of all ages
the true face of God. He said to them, "When you pray, say,"

> FATHER, HALLOWED BE YOUR NAME.
> YOUR KINGDOM COME.
> GIVE US EACH DAY OUR DAILY BREAD.
> AND FORGIVE US OUR SINS,
> FOR WE OURSELVES ALSO FORGIVE
> EVERYONE WHO IS INDEBTED TO US.
> AND LEAD US NOT INTO TEMPTATION.
> (LUKE 11:2–4 NASB)

Our Father. Familiar words, maybe so familiar that they
are no longer real. Those words were not only real, but also
revolutionary to the twelve disciples. Pagan philosophers such
as Aristotle arrived at the existence of God via human reason
and referred to Him in vague, impersonal terms: *the uncaused
cause, the immovable mover.* The prophets of Israel revealed the
God of Abraham, Isaac, and Jacob in a warmer, more compas-
sionate manner. But only Jesus revealed to an astonished Jewish
community that God is truly Father. If you took the love of
all the best mothers and fathers who have lived in the course

of human history, all their goodness, kindness, patience, fidelity, wisdom, tenderness, strength, and love and united all those qualities in a single person, that person's love would only be a faint shadow of the furious love and mercy in the heart of God the Father addressed to you and me at this moment.

We hear a beautiful echo of this in chapter 8 of Paul's letter to the Romans, where he writes:

> FOR YOU DID NOT RECEIVE A SPIRIT OF
> SLAVERY TO FALL BACK INTO FEAR, BUT
> YOU RECEIVED A SPIRIT OF ADOPTION,
> THROUGH WHICH WE CRY, "ABBA,
> FATHER!"
> (ROM. 8:15 NAB)

Abba means in literal English: daddy, papa, my own dear father.

American child psychologists tell us that the average American baby begins to speak between the ages of fourteen and eighteen months. Regardless of the sex of the child, the first word normally spoken at that age is *da*—da, da, daddy. A little Jewish child speaking Aramaic in first–century Palestine at that same age level would begin to say *ab*—ab, ab, Abba. Jesus' revelation was nothing less than a revolution. From that moment on, no Christian can ever say one form of prayer is as good as another or one religion is as good as another.

Jesus is saying that we may address the infinite, transcendent, almighty God with the intimacy, familiarity, and unshaken trust that a sixteen-month-old baby has sitting on his father's lap—*da, da, daddy*.

Is your own personal prayer life characterized by the simplicity, childlike candor, boundless trust, and easy familiarity of a little one crawling up in Daddy's lap? An assured knowing that the daddy doesn't care if the child falls asleep, starts playing with toys, or even starts chatting with little friends, because the daddy knows the child has essentially chosen to be with him for that moment? Is that the spirit of your interior prayer life?

I will never forget a retreat experience years ago in the
Midwest. It was a rather large gathering, about seven thousand people. An invitation for healing prayer followed each
night's service; I would go into a side room and meet with
those who felt compelled to come. On one particular night,
the line extended well beyond midnight and after finishing, I
went straight to bed, not even taking my clothes off I was so
exhausted. About three o'clock in the morning, I heard a rap
on the door and a squeaky little voice: "Brennan, can I talk
to you?"

I opened the door to find a seventy-eight-year-old nun.
And she began to cry.

"Sister? What can I do for you?"

We found two chairs in the hallway and her story began.

"I've never told anyone this in my entire life. It started
when I was five years old. My father would crawl into my bed
with no clothes on. He would touch me there and tell me
to touch him there; he said it's what our family doctor said
we should do. When I was nine, my father took my virgin-
ity. By the time I was twelve, I knew of every kind of sexual
perversion you read about in dirty books. Brennan, do you
have any idea how dirty I feel? I've lived with so much hatred

of my father and hatred of myself that I would only go to Communion when my absence would be conspicuous."

In the next few minutes, I prayed with her for healing. Then I asked her if she would find a quiet place every morning for the next thirty days, sit down in a chair, close her eyes, upturn her palms, and pray this one phrase over and over:

ABBA, I BELONG TO YOU.

It's a prayer of exactly seven syllables, the number that corresponds perfectly to the rhythm of our breathing. As you inhale—*Abba*. As you exhale—*I belong to You*.

Through her tears she agreed: "Yes, Brennan, I will."

One of the most moving and poetic follow-up letters I've ever received came from this sister. In it she described the inner healing of her heart, a complete forgiveness of her father, and an inner peace she'd never known in her seventy-eight years. She concluded her letter with these words:

A year ago, I would've signed this letter with my real name in religious life—Sister Mary Genevieve. But from now on, I'm Daddy's little girl.

Be aware, this is not sloppy sentimentality or indulgent wishful thinking. But rather a woman who dared to pray in the childlike trust and deep reverence that Jesus said would mark a disciple, and in doing so discovered the furious love of her Abba.

The greatest gift I've ever received in my life in Jesus is the Abba experience. I can only stutter and stammer about the life-changing power of the Abba encounter.

My name is Brennan Manning, and I'm Daddy's little boy.

In Luke's gospel, chapter 22, Jesus finally leaves the upper room and goes out into the garden of Gethsemane to give Himself over to the burden He's been carrying. Apparently, that night Jesus saw a glimpse of what it was going to cost Him to fulfill His mission as the servant of righteousness over sin. That awareness filled Jesus with such a sense of dread and terror that, as theologian Hans Kung described, "Christ was like a trapped animal in the garden clawing for some way to escape." Jesus sinks to the ground, and as Luke notes, His beads of sweat become drops of blood. At that moment, Jesus breaks into spontaneous prayer. And guess what the first word is, the very first word that arises prereflectively from Jesus' heart and mind? *Abba.*

ABBA, IF IT'S POSSIBLE,

LET THIS CUP OF PAIN PASS ME BY.

BUT LET IT BE DONE YOUR WAY, NOT MINE.

Jesus surrenders in trusting, obedient love to His Abba, and rises from the ground, no longer a trapped animal but completely at one with the Father: *atonement*—at-one-ment in the furious love God.

As Luke's story continues, Jesus is taken from Gethsemane to the high priest, who sent Him to Pilate, who sent Him to King Herod, who sent Him back to Pilate. It was Pilate who pronounced the death sentence and ordered Jesus led up to Calvary.

AND HE SAID TO THEM THE THIRD TIME,

"WHY, WHAT EVIL HAS THIS MAN DONE? I

HAVE FOUND IN HIM NO GUILT DEMANDING
DEATH; THEREFORE I WILL PUNISH HIM
AND RELEASE HIM."
BUT THEY WERE INSISTENT, WITH LOUD
VOICES ASKING THAT HE BE CRUCIFIED.
AND THEIR VOICES BEGAN TO PREVAIL.
AND PILATE PRONOUNCED SENTENCE THAT
THEIR DEMAND BE GRANTED.
(23:22–24 NASB)

The death of Jesus Christ on the cross is His greatest single act of unwavering trust in His Abba's love. He plunged into the darkness of death, not fully knowing what awaited Him, confident that somehow, some way, His Abba would vindicate Him.

Twenty years earlier, Jesus spoke these words to His panicked parents: "I must always be where My Abba is." Surely these words must have surfaced in Mary's mind as she stood at the foot of the cross watching her son die.

And then a moment in Jesus' life that is more shrouded in mystery, denser with misunderstanding and incomprehensibility than perhaps any other. Jesus, the eternally beloved Son of the Father, is abandoned by His Abba. Sin appears to have its way over the entire world. For the first time since He was an infant, Jesus feels Himself to be without the sustaining presence of His Abba, an inner bleakness of forsaken aloneness in the desolation of abandonment.

In a scream that surely split the sky:

"ELOI, ELOI, LAMA SABACHTHANI?"

"MY GOD, MY ABBA, WHY, WHY HAVE YOU FORSAKEN ME NOW?"

St. John of the Cross said it will never ever be given to any human heart to understand the depth of desolation, utter abandonment, indescribable loneliness, and complete forsakenness that lay behind Jesus' cry. But even in that cry, there is no indication that Jesus ever lost trust or hope or confidence in His Abba.

After thirty-five years of praying over the passion and death narratives in Luke's gospel, French biblical scholar Pierre Benoit believed that the Abba of Jesus spoke to His Son as He hung naked, nailed to the wood with spit dripping down His face, His body bathed in blood. And Benoit believes the words Abba spoke were words from the Hebrew Scriptures, Song of Songs 2:10–14 (NJB):

COME NOW, MY LOVE. MY LOVELY ONE,

COME.

FOR YOU, THE WINTER HAS PASSED,

THE SNOWS ARE OVER AND GONE,

THE FLOWERS APPEAR IN THE LAND,

THE SEASON OF JOYFUL SONGS HAS COME.

THE COOING OF THE TURTLEDOVE IS

HEARD IN OUR LAND.

COME NOW, MY LOVE. MY LOVELY ONE,

COME.

LET ME SEE YOUR FACE. AND LET ME HEAR
YOUR VOICE, FOR YOUR VOICE IS SWEET
AND YOUR FACE IS BEAUTIFUL.

COME NOW, MY LOVE, MY LOVELY ONE,
COME.

Abba was calling Jesus home to an intimacy of life and love that defied description, a home where every tear is wiped away, where there is no more mourning, no more sadness. And Jesus seems to hear the voice of His Abba because His last word on the cross is a response from the powerful profound intimacy of His own heart. Jesus cries:

"Abba. Abba, I'm coming. I'm coming home. Into Your hands I commend My spirit; into Your heart I commend My heart. Abba, it's finished, consummated. I'm coming home."

And the torn, broken, lacerated body of Jesus the Son is swept up into the reckless, raging fury that they call the love of God.

Since moving to New Orleans, I've gotten deeply involved in the only leper colony in the United States. It's found in Carville, Louisiana, about twenty miles southwest of Baton Rouge. I've been there many, many times. I go from room to room visiting the lepers, victims of Hansen's disease.

On one occasion, as I was coming up the front steps, a nurse came running toward me and said, "Brennan, can you come quick and pray with Yolanda? She's dying, Brennan."

I always carry the holy oils with me to anoint any who desire it. I went up to Yolanda's room on the second floor and sat on the edge of the bed. Yolanda is a woman thirty-seven years old. Five years ago, before the leprosy began to ravage, she must have been one of the most stunningly beautiful creatures God ever made. I do not mean just a cute, pretty, or even attractive woman. I mean the kind of blinding physical beauty that causes men and women on the street to stop and stare. In pictures, Yolanda had the largest, most mesmerizing, most translucent brown eyes I've ever seen, set in this exquisitely chiseled face with high cheekbones, long brown hair down to a slender waist, and a perfectly proportioned bust. But that was then.

Now her nose is pressed into her face. Her mouth is severely contorted. Both ears are distended. She has no fingers on either hand, just two little stumps. One of the first effects of leprosy is losing all sensitivity in your extremities, toes and fingers. A leper can rest her hand on a burning hot stove and feel absolutely nothing; this often leads to gangrene and eventually demands amputation. Yolanda just had these two little stumps.

Two years earlier, her husband divorced her because of the social stigma attached to leprosy, and he had forbidden their two sons, boys fourteen and sixteen, from ever visiting their mother. The father was an alcoholic, complete with frequent violent mood swings. The boys were terrified of him, so they dutifully obeyed; as a result, Yolanda was dying an abandoned, forsaken woman.

> *Those doves below, the ones utterly cared for,*
> *never endangered ones, cannot*
> *know tenderness.*
> **—Rilke**

I anointed Yolanda with oil and prayed with her. As I turned around to put the top back on the bottle of oil, the room was filled with a brilliant light. It had been raining when I came in; I didn't even look up, but said, "Thanks, Abba, for the sunshine. I bet that'll cheer her up."

As I turned to look back at Yolanda—and if I live to be three hundred years old I'll never be able to find the words to describe what I saw—her face was like a sunburst over the mountains, like one thousand sunbeams streaming out of her face literally so brilliant I had to shield my eyes.

I said, "Yolanda, you appear to be very happy."

With her slight Mexican-American accent she said, "Oh Father, I am so happy."

I then asked her, "Will you tell me why you're so happy?"

She said, "Yes, the Abba of Jesus just told me that He would take me home today."

I vividly remember the hot tears that began rolling down my cheeks. After a lengthy pause, I asked just what the Abba of Jesus said.

Yolanda said:

COME NOW, MY LOVE. MY LOVELY ONE, COME.

FOR YOU, THE WINTER HAS PASSED, THE SNOWS ARE OVER AND GONE, THE FLOWERS APPEAR IN THE LAND, THE SEASON OF JOYFUL SONGS HAS COME.

THE COOING OF THE TURTLEDOVE
IS HEARD IN OUR LAND.

COME NOW, MY LOVE. MY YOLANDA, COME.

LET ME SEE YOUR FACE. AND LET ME HEAR
YOUR VOICE, FOR YOUR VOICE IS SWEET
AND YOUR FACE IS BEAUTIFUL.

COME NOW, MY LOVE, MY LOVELY ONE,
COME.

Six hours later her little leprous body was swept up into the furious love of her Abba. Later that same day, I learned from the staff that Yolanda was illiterate. She had never read the Bible, or any book for that matter, in her entire life. I surely had never repeated those words to her in any of my visits. I was, as they say, a man undone.

CONSIDER THIS...

1. Is your personal prayer life characterized by Abba intimacy? If not, why not?

2. Prayerfully consider taking a few moments every day for the next month, closing your eyes, upturning your palms, and praying, "Abba, I belong to You." Don't make it anything more than that; trust me, it's enough.

union

Love by its nature seeks union. A skeptic would question whether union is a relevant issue as we witness the decline and fall of our culture. Is it not a trivial matter, especially in times like these? No, it is not trivial.

The sons and daughters of Abba, those living with an authentic experience of the risen Jesus, reply:

Union not only transcends every political,
social, cultural, and religious consideration
and not only infuses them with
ultimate meaning, but defines the
very purpose of life itself.

The invitation to union is extended not only for Christians of iron will, austere seekers of God, those who preach the gospel and get doctorates in theology.

> *It is not reserved for those who are*
> *well-known mystics or for those who do*
> *wonderful things for the poor.... [It is for] those*
> *poor enough to welcome Jesus. It is for people*
> *living ordinary lives and who feel lonely. It is*
> *for all those who are old, hospitalized or*
> *out of work, who open their hearts in trust*
> *to Jesus and cry out for his healing love.*[2]
> **—Jean Vanier**

I would add that the outstretched arms of Jesus exclude no one, neither the drunk in the doorway, the panhandler on the street, gays and lesbians in their isolation, the most selfish and ungrateful in their cocoons, the most unjust of employers and the most overweening of snobs. The love of Christ embraces all without exception.

Again, *the love of God is folly!*

As the brilliant contemplative Catherine de Hueck Doherty observes in *The Gospel Without Compromise*:

> *The Gospel can be summed up by saying that*
> *it is the tremendous, tender, compassionate,*
> *gentle, extraordinary, explosive,*
> *revolutionary revelation of Christ's love.*

I HAVE GIVEN THEM THE GLORY YOU GAVE TO ME, THAT THEY MAY BE ONE AS WE ARE ONE. WITH ME IN THEM AND YOU IN ME, MAY THEY BE SO PERFECTED IN UNITY THAT THE WORLD WILL RECOGNIZE THAT IT WAS YOU WHO SENT ME AND THAT YOU HAVE LOVED THEM AS YOU HAVE LOVED ME. (JOHN 17:22–23 NJB)

While praying over those remarkable words, I came to the inescapable conclusion that the degree of Abba's love for me is in direct proportion to His love for Jesus. For example, I can love the mailman with twenty percent and my best friend with ninety percent. But with God, there is no division, no more and no less. God loves me as much as He loves Jesus. Wow!

❈   ❈   ❈   ❈   ❈

Catherine of Siena was one of three women in the Catholic tradition honored with the title Doctor of Theology because of her personal holiness and the depth of her writing on the spiritual life. She prayed:

> *When then, eternal Father, did you create this*
> *creature of yours?...You show me that you made*
> *us for one reason only: in your light you saw*
> *yourself compelled by the fire of your love to give*
> *us being in spite of the evil we would commit*
> *against you, eternal Father. It was fire, then,*
> *that compelled you. Oh, unutterable love, even*
> *though you saw all the evils your creatures*
> *would commit against your infinite goodness,*
> *you acted as if you did not see and set your*

eye only on the beauty of your creature, with
whom you had fallen in love like one drunk and
crazy with love.... You are the fire, nothing but
a fire of love, crazy over what you have made.
—The Prayers of Catherine of Siena

I believe that only a person who has actually experienced God (a mystic) would dare to pray with such boldness. An inner, transcendent experience was the foundation of her audacious prayer. In another of my books, *Ruthless Trust*, I have discussed our urgent need for artists, mystics, and clowns. Even the most profound intellectual insights fail to foster intrepid prayer, like Catherine's colorful invocation— "Oh, Divine Madman ..."

The only cure for the angst of modern man
is mysticism.
—Thomas Merton

I began reading Thomas Brodie's commentary on the gospel of John on the recommendation of my spiritual director, Vince Hovley. And Vince got into it because a Christian scholar whom he greatly admires, Jean Vanier, wrote that of all the numerous commentaries on John, Brodie's was the most helpful.

Brodie argues persuasively that the starting point of John's theology is *abiding restful union*. The Irish scholar first establishes the union of Jesus with His Father. The prologue speaks of Jesus being "in the bosom of the Father" (1:1, 18). As the gospel progresses, Jesus speaks not only of His oneness with the Father, but also of His union with us. "Make your home in me just as I do in you" (15:4 MSG). The extraordinary picture of the beloved reclining on Jesus' breast (13:23–25) and John's surprising repetition of that intimate moment at the very end of his gospel (21:20) convey the intention that abiding restful union frames his gospel.

Brodie writes:

Thus there is a form of restful union
which exists first of all in God, but in which
humans can participate both during
this life and during a later life.

Words such as *union*, *fusion*, and *symbiosis* hint at the ineffable oneness with Jesus that the apostle Paul experienced: "It is no longer I who live, but Christ lives in me" (Gal. 2:20). No human word is even remotely adequate to convey the mysterious and furious longing of Jesus for you and me to live in His smile and hang on His words. But *union* comes close, very close; it is a word pregnant with a reality that surpasses understanding, the only reality worth yearning for with love and patience, the only reality before which we should stay very quiet.

> CEASE STRIVING AND KNOW THAT
> I AM GOD.
> (PS. 46:10 NASB)

After reading Brodie, I've decided that if I had my life to live over again, I would not only climb more mountains, swim more rivers, and watch more sunsets; I wouldn't only jettison my hot water bottle, raincoat, umbrella, parachute, and raft; I would not only go barefoot earlier in the spring and stay out later in the fall; but I would devote not one more minute to monitoring my spiritual growth. No, not one.

Gerald May is incisive and humorous:

> *The entire process (of self-development) can be*
> *very exciting and entertaining. But the problem*
> *is there's no end to it. The fantasy is that if one*
> *heads in the right direction and just works hard*
> *enough to learn new things and grows enough*
> *and gets actualized, one will be there. None of*
> *us is quite certain exactly where there is, but it*
> *obviously has something to do with resting.*[3]

In retrospect, my ponderous ponderings on the purgative, illuminative, and unitive stages of my spiritual life, my assiduous search for shortcuts to holiness, my preoccupation with my spiritual pulse and my fasts, mortifications, and penances have wrought pseudobliss and the egregious delusion that I was securely ensconced in the seventh mansion of spiritual perfection.

What would I actually do if I had it to do all over again? Heeding John's counsel, I would simply do the next thing in love.

Unlike the Synoptic Gospels, John recognizes the divinity of Jesus in the very first sentence of his gospel: "In the beginning was the Word." The experience of recognition has proved decisive in my life; the immediate cause of psychological and spiritual change. As biblical scholar John McKenzie explains:

> *We recognize that the person whom we have encountered speaks to our innermost being, supplies our needs, satisfies our desires. We recognize that this person gives life meaning. I do not say a new meaning simply, for we realize that before we encountered this person life had no real meaning. We recognize that this person has revealed to us not only himself, but our own true self as well. We recognize that we cannot be our own true self except by union with this person. In him, the obscure is illuminated,*

the uncertain yields to the certain, insecurity
is replaced by a deep sense of security. In him
we find we have achieved an understanding of
many things which baffled us. We recognize in
his person strength and power which we can
sense passing from him to us. Most certainly,
if most obscurely, we recognize that in this
person we have encountered God, and that we
shall not encounter God in any other way.[4]

Once again, love by its nature seeks union. With the grace of recognition comes the awesome and alarming awareness that Jesus, the incarnation of the furious longing of God, wants more than a close relationship with you and me; He seeks nothing less than *union*. The myriad implications of such oneness mean different things on different days. Sitting before the computer at this moment, it means living in His smile and hanging on His every word.

Leaving for a moment his ivory tower of exegesis, the disciplined wild man Brodie grows lyrical:

Oneness with ultimate reality is not an abstract idea; it is a spiritual experience of knowing that the timeless God is at the door inviting you to full union. It is an attentiveness to the present, a readiness, at every moment, to receive reality, to enjoy deeply even the simplest things. In the words of poet Paul Murray: "This moment, the grace of this one raptureless moment ..."[5]

CONSIDER THIS...

1. How often do you monitor your spiritual growth—
   Several times a day? Once a month? Every thirty
   days? Twice a year?

2. Would you, could you, devote not one more minute
   to monitoring your spiritual growth? If so, it's
   possible you just might find you like green eggs and
   ham.

unplanned
moment of prayer

Jesus, human words cannot bear the weight of Your mercy and compassion. My union with You is like being so attached that life seems impossible without You. Detached from You during my days of sour wine and withered roses was a shadow life. I have no sense of myself apart from You. My bones say thank You for this now moment. Amen.

The ordinary pablum of popular religion caters to the idealistic, perfectionistic, and neurotic self who fixates on graceless getting worthy for union, while allowing the prostitutes and tax gougers to dance into the kingdom. Our strategies of self-deception persuade us that abiding restful union with Jesus is too costly, leaving no room for money, ambition, success, fame, sex, power, control, and pride of place or the fatal trap of self-rejection, thus prohibiting mediocre, disaffected dingbats and dirtballs, like myself, from intimacy with Jesus.

Until we learn to live peacefully with what Andre Louf calls "our amazing degree of weakness," until we learn to live gracefully with what Alan Jones calls "our own extreme psychic frailty," until we let the Christ who consorted with hookers and crooks to be our truth, the false, fraudulent self motivated by cowardice and fear will continue to distance us from *abiding restful union.*

Young Christians are sick of pablum. It doesn't work anymore. They are tired of rabbinical hair-splitting, empty liturgical apparatus, Sunday school minutiae, the ghostly voices of the old regime; they reject stuck minds and methods and by their indifference to structures and traditional authorities have declared them bankrupt, cancelled.

Listening to evangelical college students over the past twenty years, I hear them asking a different and salient question, a question in which the law and prophets are summed up like nothing else:

Are we responding to the love of Jesus
living within us concretely and consistently
in our love for one another?

There are no palliatives for raw faith. In living out our union with Jesus one day at a time, the most decisive issue is *believing*. In contrast to the domesticated, feel-good Jesus of TV evangelism, who is committed to our financial prosperity, the Christ of John's gospel who has made His home in us invites us to walk with Him daily in humble service even unto death. We may have acquired graduate degrees; we may have mastered biblical principles; we may hold roles of secular and spiritual leadership; and we may have authored books on Christian maturity; and our wits may have been sharpened on the Carborundum wheel of the world. So much the better if they have elicited raw faith, so much the worse for those on the inside track who dismiss *union*, *fusion*, and *symbiosis* as merely sophisticated metaphors not to be taken literally.

Believing is living as though John 15:4 is true.

ABIDE IN ME, AND I IN YOU. AS THE
BRANCH CANNOT BEAR FRUIT OF ITSELF
UNLESS IT ABIDES IN THE VINE, SO NEITHER
CAN YOU UNLESS YOU ABIDE IN ME.

It is sad to say, but the familiar phrase "the unconditional love of God" has become cliché, a true but trite expression devoid of any real meaning. Words, like anything else used too often, soon depreciate in value, lose their edge, and cease to bite into our lives. When phrases, such as *unconditional love*, trip too easily off the tongue, the speaker's ego may experience a temporary rush of exhilaration using an *in* salvation slogan, but his heart remains unchanged.

How do I know this? Well, I have long been smitten with concepts. They engage my mind, rustle my thought process, and stir my emotions. *Unconditional love* as a concept has transported me to intellectual nirvana, motivated the reading of at least fifty books on related themes, and deluded me into believing that I was *there*. Until along came a day when I was appalled to discover that nothing had changed. It was all a head trip. Lofty thoughts and impersonal concepts left my lousy self-image intact and my way of praying unchanged.

Until the love of God that knows no boundary, limit, or breaking point is internalized through personal decision; until the furious longing of God seizes the imagination; until the heart is conjoined to the mind through sheer grace, nothing happens. The idolatry of ideas has left me puffed up, narrow-minded, and intolerant of any idea that does not coincide with mine.

The wild, unrestricted love of God is not simply an inspiring idea. When it imposes itself on mind and heart with the stark reality of ontological truth, it determines why and at what time you get up in the morning, how you pass your evenings, how you spend your weekends, what you read, and who you hang with; it affects what breaks your heart, what amazes you, and what makes your heart happy.

The revolutionary thinking that God loves me as I am and not as I should be requires radical rethinking and profound emotional readjustment. Small wonder that the late spiritual giant

Basil Hume of London, England, claimed that Christians find it easier to believe that God exists than that God loves them.

In his magnificent book *God First Loved Us*, Antony Campbell remarks:

> *Originally, I believed the acceptance of a loving*
> *God involved a sufficient but relative minor*
> *shift of attitude. After all, it was on so many*
> *people's lips. The more I worked with it, the*
> *more I realize that the acceptance in faith of*
> *God's unconditional love was not only hugely*
> *significant, it required a major change of*
> *attitude ... the major shift may be the images*
> *we have of God and ourselves. How radically is*
> *our image of God reshaped if we take seriously*
> *the belief in God as deeply, passionately, and*
> *unconditionally loving us? How radically must*
> *we rework our own self-image if we accept*
> *ourselves as loveable—as deeply, passionately,*
> *and unconditionally loved by God?*[6]

Two important corollaries flow from this life-changing revolution. First, if we continue to picture God as a small-minded bookkeeper, a niggling customs officer rifling through our moral suitcase, as a policeman with a club who is going to bat us over the head every time we stumble and fall, or as a whimsical, capricious, and cantankerous thief who delights in raining on our parade and stealing our joy, we flatly deny what John writes in his first letter (4:16)—"God is love." In human beings, love is a quality, a high-prized virtue; in God, love is His identity.

Secondly, if we continue to view ourselves as moral lepers and spiritual failures, if our lives are shadowed by low self-esteem, shame, remorse, unhealthy guilt, and self-hatred, we reject the teaching of Jesus and cling to our negative self-image.

In the fifth century, St. Augustine wrote this lyrical line:

> *Quia amasti me, fecisti me amabilem.*
> *(In loving me, you made me lovable.)*

little gifts

If there were ever words written by another author for which I would swap every one of my own, they would be the words of the following paragraph by Hans Urs Von Balthasar:

I say to you, Blessed is he who exposes himself
to an existence never brought under mastery,
who does not transcend, but rather abandons
himself to my ever-transcending grace. Blessed
are not the enlightened whose every question
has been answered and who are delighted
with their own sublime insight, the mature
and ripe ones whose one remaining action is
to fall from the tree. Blessed, rather, are the

chased, the harassed who must daily stand
before my enigmas and cannot solve them.
Blessed are the poor in spirit, those who lack a
spirit of cleverness. Woe to the rich, and woe to
the doubly rich in spirit! Although nothing is
impossible with God, it is difficult for the Spirit
to move their fat hearts. The poor are willing
and easy to direct. Like little puppies they do not
take their eyes from their master's hand to see
if perhaps he may throw them a little morsel
from his plate. So carefully do the poor follow
my promptings that they listen to the wind
(which blows where it pleases), even when
it changes. From the sky they can read the
weather and interpret the signs of the times.
My grace is unpretentious, but the poor
are satisfied with little gifts.[7]

healing

A few years back I was the featured speaker at the Indiana Governor's Prayer Breakfast. I found myself sitting with the then youngest (thirty-six years old) governor in the country, Evan Bayh. He's also a very devout Christian. He turned to me and said, "Brennan, you're in just about every nook and cranny of the United States. You're in every college and university, from Campus Crusade to Young Life, and in an incredible number of churches as well. What do you hear the Spirit of God saying to the American church?"

I said, "Well, Governor Bayh, if there's one thing I hear with growing clarity, it's that God is calling each and every Christian to personally participate in the healing ministry of Jesus Christ."

Healing is a response to a crisis in the life of another person. It's enough of a response, a satisfactory response to a crisis in the life of another. And wherever the word *crisis* is used in the Greek New Testament, it is translated in English as *judgment*. That's right—*judgment*. Healing is a response that I make to a decisive moment in the life of a brother or sister; whether I respond or not, I have made a judgment.

Healing becomes the opportunity to pass off to another human being what I have received from the Lord Jesus; namely His unconditional acceptance of me as I am, not as I should be. He loves me whether in a state of grace or disgrace, whether I live up to the lofty expectations of His gospel or I don't. He comes to me where I live and loves me as I am.

When I have passed that same reality on to another human being, the result most often has been the inner healing of their heart through the touch of my affirmation. To affirm a person is to see the good in them that they cannot see in themselves and to repeat it in spite of appearances to the contrary. Please, this is not some Pollyanna optimism that is blind to the reality of evil, but rather like a fine radar system that is tuned in to the true, the good, and the beautiful. When a person is evoked for who she is, not who she is not, the most often result will be the inner healing of her heart through the touch of affirmation.

> FINALLY, BRETHREN, WHATEVER IS TRUE,
> WHATEVER IS HONORABLE, WHATEVER
> IS RIGHT, WHATEVER IS PURE, WHATEVER
> IS LOVELY, WHATEVER IS OF GOOD REPUTE,
> IF THERE IS ANY EXCELLENCE AND
> IF ANYTHING WORTHY OF PRAISE,
> DWELL ON THESE THINGS.
> (PHIL. 4:8 NASB)

When you read the Gospels carefully, you notice this extraordinary gift that Jesus had. I'm not talking about physical healing per se, but more of the inner healing through a simple word, a look, a glance, a touch. Consider the celebrated scene with the little runt Zacchaeus. He's collecting taxes for Rome from his own people, with a kickback from the take. He's a traitor to the Jewish cause and the Jews are on to him, so they excommunicate him, a terrible penalty at the time. Basically, it meant that Zacchaeus, a lifelong Jew, could never again eat a meal in a Jewish home. He could never go to the synagogue on the Sabbath or to Jerusalem for the high feast.

One day Zacchaeus is in his shop counting his money and he hears the prophet of Nazareth is passing by. He wants to get a look, so he runs down the street. Now remember, this is Zacchaeus, the wee little man. He's so short he can't see over the shoulders of the taller men, so he climbs up a sycamore tree. Interesting, isn't it? He went out on a limb for Jesus.

Jesus looks up and says, "Zacchaeus, come down. I want to have supper in your house today."

Now, when an orthodox Jew, which Jesus was, says "I want to have supper with you," he's saying, *I want to enter into friendship with you.* Everyone else in that self-righteous, judgmental, Jewish community drove deeper and deeper into isolation, deciding to put up with Zacchaeus just as he was. But Jesus looked at him and believed in what he could become, so He invited Himself to dinner.

And what happens? Zacchaeus jumps down out of the tree. Feelings that were dried up for years in his heart suddenly began to well up, boil up, convert his entire being. He begins to blubber, "Uh, Uh, I'll give back fourfold everything I've stolen. And I'll give half my goods to the poor." Jesus' affirming "Come down" changed the direction of the wee little man's life.

Is there a Zacchaeus in your life? Somebody that everybody's given up on? Judged incapable of any further good? Grandaunt, distant cousin, spouse, former spouse, in-law, member of your church, neighbor on your street, colleague at work? Someone of whom you've said, "I've been wasting my time trying to make you understand anything. You are incorrigible. Thank God, I'm quits and free of you. Don't you ever dare to darken my door again"? You probably wouldn't say that because that's cruel. I don't like to say cruel things either. They make me feel guilty and I don't want to feel guilty. So, I play it smooth; I call it cool cordiality and polite indifference. *Good morning, you dork.* In the churches across our land, we allow this garbage to masquerade as the love of Jesus.

Jesus said you are to love one another as I have loved you, a love that will possibly lead to the bloody, anguished gift of yourself; a love that forgives seventy times seven, that keeps no score of wrongdoing. Jesus said this, this love, is the one criterion, the sole norm, the standard of discipleship in the New Israel of God. He said you're going to be identified as His disciples, not because of your church-going, Bible-toting, or song-singing. No, you'll be identified as His by one sign only: the deep and delicate respect for one another, the cordial love impregnated with reverence for the sacred dimension of the human personality because of the mysterious substitution of Christ for the Christian.

Matthew 25:34 (NASB) says that the King will say, "Come, you who are blessed of My Father, inherit the kingdom prepared for you from the foundation of the world." He tells me that I'm blessed, beloved, beautiful, and pleasing to the eyes of my Abba to the extent that I've become a beneficiary of the

kingdom. Why? Not because I shouted, "Jesus is Lord," but because someone was hungry and I gave him food. Somebody was thirsty and I gave her a drink. I welcomed the stranger, clothed the naked, comforted the sick, and visited the prisoner. On that day, many of us will protest, "Lord, when?" And then comes the revelation of revelations, the end of the greatest story ever told, when Jesus looks into my eyes and says, "What you did to them, you did to Me; as often as for one of the least of My brothers and sisters, so to Me."

What is the sign, par excellence, of authentic discipleship? The night before Jesus died, He left no doubt in anybody's mind. "A new commandment I give to you, that you love one another, even as I have loved you … By this all men will know" (John 13:34–35 NASB).

The apostle Paul may have understood the mind of Jesus better than anyone who ever lived. He sums up his whole understanding of the message of Jesus in Galatians 5:6 when he writes, "the only thing that matters is the faith that expresses itself in love." According to Paul's criterion for greatness in the New Israel of God, the person who is the most Christlike, closest to the heart of Abba, is not the one who spends the most time in prayer. It's not the one who has the most PhDs. It's not the one who has the most responsibility entrusted to his care. It's not the pastor of the biggest megachurch. No, it's the one who loves the most. That's not my opinion. Those are the words in Galatians 5 that will judge us.

According to that mysterious substitution of Christ for the Christian, what we do to one another we do to Jesus. What would Jesus do to the Zacchaeus in your life and mine? He'd pause, look at them, and love them with such disarming simplicity, such unaccustomed tenderness, and such infectious joy that He'd wring from their calloused hearts real bursts of joy, gratitude, and wonder. Jesus expected the most of every man and woman; and behind their grumpiest poses, their most puzzling defense mechanisms, their coarseness, their arrogance, their dignified airs, their silence, and their sneers and curses, Jesus sees a little child who wasn't loved enough—a *least of these* who had ceased growing because someone had ceased believing in them.

How have we gotten it so screwed up?

I was speaking to the Navigators not long ago and they asked, "Do you have a word for us?"

I said, "Yes, I do. Instead of being identified as a community that memorizes Scripture, why not be identified as a community of professional lovers that causes people to say 'How they love one another!'" Why do we judge Jesus' criterion for authentic discipleship irrelevant? Jesus said the world is going to recognize you as His by only one sign: the way you are with one another on the street every day. You are going to leave people feeling a little better or a little worse. You're going to affirm them or deprive them, but there'll be no neutral exchange. If we as a Christian community took seriously that the sign of our love for Jesus is our love for one another, I am convinced it would change the world. We're denying to the world the one witness Jesus asked for:

LOVE ONE ANOTHER
AS I'VE LOVED YOU.
(JOHN 15:12)

Back in the late 1960s, I was teaching at a university in Ohio and there was a student on campus who by society's standards would've been called ugly. He was short, extremely obese, he had a terrible case of acne, a bad lisp, and his hair was growing like Lancelot's horse—in four directions at one time. He wore the uniform of the day: a T-shirt that hadn't been washed since the Spanish American War, jeans with a butterfly on the back, and of course, no shoes.

In all my days, I have never met anybody with such low self-esteem. He told me that when he looked in the mirror each morning, he spit at it. Of course no campus girl would date him. No fraternity wanted him as a pledge.

He walked into my office one day and said, his lisp evident, "Ah, you're a new face on campus. Well, my name is Larry Malaney and I'm an athgnostic."

I said, "*You're what?*"

He repeated himself and I said, "Wow, congratulations! If you ever become an atheist, I'll take you to dinner and we'll celebrate your conversion."

The story I'm about to tell you is what Larry got for Christmas one year.

Christmas came along for Larry Malaney and he found himself back with his parents in Providence, Rhode Island. Larry's father is a typical lace-curtain Irishman. Now there are lace-curtain Irish and there are shanty Irish. A lace-curtain Irishman, even on the hottest day in summer, will not come to the dining room table without wearing a suit, usually a dark pinstripe, starched white shirt, and a tie swollen at the top. He will never allow his sideburns to grow to the top of his ears and he always speaks in a low, subdued voice.

Well, Larry comes to the dinner table that first night home, smelling like a Billy goat. He and his father have the usual number of quarrels and reconciliations. And thus begins a typical vacation in the Malaney household. Several nights later, Larry tells his father that he's got to get back to school the next day.

"What time, son?"

"Six o'clock."

"Well, I'll ride the bus with you."

The next morning, the father and son ride the bus in silence. They get off the bus, as Larry has to catch a second one to get to the airport. Directly across the street are six men standing

under an awning, all men who work in the same textile fac-
tory as Larry's father. They begin making loud and degrading
remarks like "Oink, oink, look at that fat pig. I tell you, if that
pig was my kid, I'd hide him in the basement, I'd be so embar-
rassed." Another said, "I wouldn't. If that slob was my kid, he'd
be out the door so fast, he wouldn't know if he's on foot or
horseback. Hey, pig! Give us your best oink!"

These brutal salvos continued.

Larry Malaney told me that in that moment, for the first time
in his life, his father reached out and embraced him, kissed him on
the lips, and said, "Larry, if your mother and I live to be two hundred years old, that wouldn't be long enough to thank God for the
gift He gave to us in you. I am so proud that you're my son!"

It would be hard to describe in words the transformation
that took place in Larry Malaney, but I'll try. He came back to
school and remained a hippie, but he cleaned up the best he could.
Miracle of miracles, Larry began dating a girl. And to top it off, he
became the president of one of the fraternities. By the way, he was
the first student in the history of our university to graduate with a
4.2 grade point average. Larry Malaney had a brilliant mind.

Larry came to my office one day and said, "Tell me about this
man Jesus." And for the next six weeks, in half-hour increments,

I shared with Larry what the Holy Spirit had revealed to me about Jesus. At the end of those six weeks, Larry said, "Okay."

June 14, 1974, Larry Malaney was ordained a priest in the diocese of Providence, Rhode Island. And for the past twenty years, he's been a missionary in South America, a man totally sold out to Jesus Christ. Do you know why? It wasn't because of the six weeks of sitting in Brennan Manning's office while I talked about Jesus. No, it was because of a day, long ago, during a Christmas vacation, standing at a bus stop, when his lace-curtain Irish father healed him. Yes, his father healed him. His father had the guts to get out of the foxhole and choose the high road of blessing in the face of cursing and taunts. His father looked deeply into his son's eyes, saw the good in Larry Malaney that Larry couldn't see for himself, affirmed him with a furious love, and changed the whole direction of his son's life.

Lodged in your heart is the power to walk into somebody's life and give him or her what the bright Paul Tillich called "the courage to be." Can you fathom that? You have the power to give someone *the courage to be*, simply by the touch of your affirmation. This might mean that you need to reach out a hand of reconciliation to someone you've estranged. It might mean making a telephone call to somebody with whom you've had a conflict. It might mean making a long-distance phone call to someone in your family that you haven't talked to in years. It might mean inviting a work colleague, whom you can't stand, out to lunch or dinner.

PEOPLE WERE BRINGING LITTLE CHILDREN TO HIM, FOR HIM TO TOUCH THEM. THE DISCIPLES SCOLDED THEM, BUT WHEN JESUS SAW THIS HE WAS INDIGNANT AND SAID TO THEM "LET THE LITTLE CHILDREN COME TO ME; DO NOT STOP THEM, FOR IT IS TO SUCH AS THESE THAT THE KINGDOM OF GOD BELONGS. IN TRUTH I TELL YOU, ANYONE WHO DOES NOT WELCOME THE KINGDOM OF GOD LIKE A LITTLE CHILD WILL NEVER ENTER IT." THEN HE EMBRACED THEM, LAID HIS HANDS ON THEM AND GAVE THEM HIS BLESSING.

(MARK 10:13–16 NJB)

Back in the late '70s, I was living in a monastery in Philadelphia. Some millionaire friends from New York City called and asked if I'd like to come up to the city for the week, go to a play on Broadway, eat at Sardi's. This, dear reader, was not a hard decision to make.

One evening we went to a play, and after the first act we went out in the street for intermission. The tuxedoed husbands got into a dense discussion with their bejeweled, evening-gowned wives on the influence of the German philosopher Schopenhauer on Samuel Beckett's "Theatre of the Absurd." Obviously, they asked me what I thought. I was about to deliver an observation so profound that it would render the discussion moot for eternity, when she walked by.

She was not one of the beautiful people. She wore a cab driver's cap, double-breasted man's suit with the pockets ripped out, holes in her nylons, and tennis shoes.

As she approached, I noticed she was peddling *Variety* newspapers, the show biz paper. In those days, it cost seventy-five cents. So, in a gesture of great generosity, I reached in my pocket, handed her a dollar, and waved her away, and then returned to my wealthy friends awaiting my next astute observation on the absurd.

And then she said, "Father?" In those days, I knew I couldn't distinguish myself by my virtues, so I distinguished myself by my clothing; I always wore the collar.

"Father, could I talk to you a minute?"

I snapped, "What? Can't you see I'm busy? Do you make a habit of interrupting people in the middle of a conversation? Wait over there and I'll speak to you when I'm done."

She whispered, "Jesus wouldn't talk to Mary Magdalene like that."

And then she was gone.

I'd treated the woman like she was a thing, like a vending machine you put your money in, and out comes your choice. I'd shown no appreciation at all for the little service that she was performing. No interest whatsoever in the little drama of her daily things. Not one ounce of cordial love impregnated with respect for the sacred dimension of her personality. Frankly, I was so caught up in trying to impress my millionaire friends with how aesthetically brilliant I was that I missed her. If she had even a sliver of a negative self-image when she approached me, I had made a mountain out of molehill.

Now let's suppose, just suppose, that this woman came to church on Sunday and there was Brennan Manning, in the

pulpit, exhorting her to believe that God loves her uncon-
ditionally as she is and not as she should be. My hypocrisy
outside the Shepherd Theatre that night made the theatre of
the absurd look inviting. How could she believe in the love of a
God she can't see when she couldn't find even a trace of love in
the eyes of a brother wearing a clerical collar whom she could
see? A shriveled humanity has a shrunken capacity for receiving
the rays of God's love.

*And they'll know we are Christians by our love, by our love, yes
they'll know we are Christians by our love.* Or not.

I know of no illustration of healing through affirmation that's
more powerful than in the dialogue between Don Quixote
and Aldonsa in the musical *Man of La Mancha*. A popular
film version was released in 1972 starring Peter O'Toole and
Sophia Loren; both musical and film were based on Miguel de
Cervantes' *Don Quixote*. If you're not familiar with the story,
Aldonsa is a trollop. She's slept with every man in the prison,

sometimes for money, sometimes just for sheer pleasure. As a result, she's lost every trace of self-respect. She's filled with overwhelming guilt and self-hatred because of her promiscuous sexual life.

And then one day along comes Don Quixote, striding utterly unselfishly into her life. He befriends her and begins to woo her by infusing into her life a sense of dignity, worth, and purpose. All his efforts are in vain. She rebuffs him at every turn. Still he pursues, calling her by the Latin *Dulcinea*, meaning *my sweet little one*. At other times, he calls her *My Lady*, to give her a sense of aristocratic bearing.

Don Quixote describes her appearance in the following terms:

> ... her name is Dulcinea, her country El Toboso,
> a village of La Mancha, her rank must be at
> least that of a princess, since she is my queen
> and lady, and her beauty superhuman, since
> all the impossible and fanciful attributes of
> beauty which the poets apply to their ladies
> are verified in her; for her hairs are gold, her
> forehead Elysian fields, her eyebrows rainbows,

her eyes suns, her cheeks roses, her lips coral,
her teeth pearls, her neck alabaster, her bosom
marble, her hands ivory, her fairness snow, and
what modesty conceals from sight such,
I think and imagine, as rational reflection
can only extol, not compare.[8]

One day, he calls out both names: "Dulcinea, My Lady!" She takes off her apron and comes storming into the room, seething with contempt. She then begins her litany of self-hatred, a once-and-for-all attempt to distance herself from any notion of a *lady*. I'll paraphrase her speech:

She was abandoned by her mother after a less than desirable birth. If she'd had a lady's sense, she would have given up and died, right there in the ditch. But she didn't.

A lady would gladly point to her father, but with a sweeping arm of shame, she'd have to include the men of an entire regiment. Ladies see themselves in their father's eyes. She sees nothing.

A delicate birth could have dictated an upright life. But much of her time is spent flat on her back; the kitchen whore men casually use then discard.

She rails at Don Quixote to see her as she really is, not the lady of his dreams. She has learned to live a life of harsh realities, life as it is; she survives by taking and then dishing it back. His eyes clouded with *could-be* drive her to despair.

> *Blows and abuse I can take and give back*
> *again, but tenderness I cannot bear.*

Her speech concludes with her vision of herself: "I'm just a whore."

But again and again, Don Quixote returns. And in spite of all appearances to the contrary, he sees what is true, good, and beautiful in Aldonsa. And slowly, from the way she sees herself reflected in the eyes of the old knight, she begins to remember.

> *I only know the dying heart needs the*
> *nourishment of memory*
> *to live beyond too many winters.*
> **—Rod McKuen**

And slowly that other Don Quixote, Jesus the Christ, begins to stride before her eyes, saying, "The past is over and done. We all stumble on the way to maturity. We all look for love in the wrong arms, happiness in the wrong places. But out of it, you've become real. You've got a heart of immense compassion for the brokenness of others. You are utterly incapable of hypocrisy, and I am deeply in love with you."

In the musical version, a most powerful moment comes when Aldonsa leaves the stage and walks down into the first row of the audience and proudly announces: "From this day forward my name is no longer Aldonsa. I am Dulcinea."

FOR ZION'S SAKE I WILL NOT
KEEP SILENT,

AND FOR JERUSALEM'S SAKE I WILL
NOT KEEP QUIET,

UNTIL HER RIGHTEOUSNESS GOES
FORTH LIKE BRIGHTNESS,

AND HER SALVATION LIKE A TORCH
THAT IS BURNING.

The nations will see your
righteousness,

And all kings your glory;
And you will be called by a new name,

Which the mouth of the Lord
will designate.
(Is. 62:1–2 nasb)

How would you describe what happened to that woman? The words I would use are *born again, recreated, renewed, healed* by the loving touch of Don Quixote's furious love.

But then, in one of those tragic ironies of life, Don Quixote falls desperately ill. His mind is weary from thinking too much, his heart is broken from having loved too much, and his body is spent from having fought too much. He lies on his bed in a semicoma. Aldonsa, now Dulcinea, comes and kneels beside him and plunges into the healing ministry of Jesus Christ.

What did the Lord say the night before He died? If any one of you loves Me, you'll be true to My word and My Abba will love you, will come to you, and make a home within you. Jesus spoke of the life of Grace, amazing Grace, not as some theological abstraction or concept; for Jesus, Grace was relationship, the presence of Abba Himself in our hearts through the gift of the Holy Spirit.

This is the same healing spirit that dwells in the human soul of Jesus Christ that enables the blind to see, the deaf to hear, and the lame to walk again. That's the identical healing spirit that dwelt in the great soul of Larry Malaney's father, empowering him to resurrect his son to newness of life. It's the same healing spirit dwelling in the great soul of Aldonsa, now Dulcinea. The question is not *can she heal?* There's only one healer in the New Israel of God and that is Jesus the Christ. The only question is *will she allow the healing spirit of the risen Jesus to flow through her; will she reach out, and touch Him?*

Aldonsa, now Dulcinea, stays by his side, imploring him to wake and remember. She longs for his voice, the furious voice of love that spoke that one word—*Dulcinea.*

The knight of the woeful countenance hears that one word and gently wakes. He scratches his head, trying to sweep the cobwebs from his mind of what must have been just a dream. But then it is Dulcinea's turn to speak the words of *could-be;* words that dream against words like *unbeatable, unbearable, unrightable, unreachable,* and *impossible.*

Her voice and words rekindle the flame in the old knight. Her glory calls him to rise—Don Quixote, the Man of La Mancha.

He stumbles out of his bed reborn, recreated, renewed, healed. He is born again by the loving touch of Dulcinea's affirmation and to the end he will dream his impossible dream.

The question is not *can we heal?* The question, the only question, is *will we let the healing power of the risen Jesus flow through us to reach and touch others, so that they may dream and fight and bear and run where the brave dare not go?*

CONSIDER THIS...

1. Ask the Father to bring to your mind one person in your life who has administered the healing touch of Jesus to you. Spend a few minutes in gratitude.

2. Now ask the Father to bring to your mind one person in your life who needs that same healing touch. Take some time and decide on a tangible way you can return the favor.

boldness

The New Oxford English Dictionary contains thirty words from the Yiddish vocabulary; words like *kibitz, kibbutz, goy, mensch,* and of course, *chutzpah.*

chutzpah—*Function: noun*

Etymology: Yiddish khutspe,
from Late Hebrew huspāh

supreme self-confidence, boldness, nerve,
sometimes an obnoxious aggressiveness.

Esther Schwartz was in front of a hotel in Miami with her three-year-old grandson, Jacob. She absolutely adores Jacob. She bought precious little Jacob a canary yellow circular sun-hat so the sun wouldn't touch the top of Jacob's head. She also bought him a pail and shovel. Out on the beach, Esther marvels at Jacob's grace: picking up the sand, putting it in the pail, picking up more sand, putting more sand in the pail.

Oh, Yahweh, thank You so much for Jacob.

Just then a tremendous wave comes in, picks up little Jacob, pail and shovel, and washes them out to sea. Esther Schwartz is very upset. She looks up at the sky and shouts, "Who do You think You are? Do You know who I am? I am Esther Schwartz. My husband, Solomon Schwartz, is a physician, and my son, Billy Schwartz, is a dentist. How dare You do that?"

Just then, a second tremendous tidal wave washes little Jacob, pail and shovel, right back to his grandmother's feet. Esther Schwartz looks up at the sky and shouts, "He had a canary yellow hat. Where's the hat?"

That, my friends, is *chutzpah*.

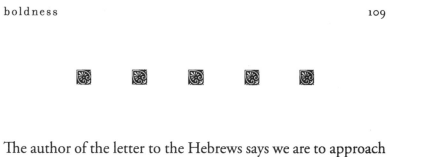

The author of the letter to the Hebrews says we are to approach
the throne of grace with *chutzpah*, knowing we will find mercy
and grace in time of need.

already ours, claim it because it has been given

THEREFORE LET US DRAW NEAR WITH
CONFIDENCE TO THE THRONE OF GRACE, SO
THAT WE MAY RECEIVE MERCY AND FIND
GRACE TO HELP IN TIME OF NEED.

(4:16 NASB)

THEREFORE, BRETHREN, SINCE WE HAVE
CONFIDENCE TO ENTER THE HOLY PLACE BY THE
BLOOD OF JESUS, BY A NEW AND LIVING WAY
WHICH HE INAUGURATED FOR US THROUGH
THE VEIL, THAT IS, HIS FLESH, AND SINCE
WE HAVE A GREAT PRIEST OVER THE HOUSE
OF GOD, LET US DRAW NEAR WITH A SINCERE
HEART IN FULL ASSURANCE OF FAITH.

= confidence

(10:19–22 NASB)

And this from the *Book of Common Prayer*, 1559 edition:

... also that I may with a <u>free conscience</u> and
<u>quiet hert</u>, in all manner of temptations,
afflictions, or necessities, and even in the
verie pangs of death, <u>crie boldly and merily</u>
unto thee, and say: I beleve in God the Father
Almightie, maker of heaven and earth.

seem opposite, but equal

Years ago the professional golfer Arnold Palmer played a series of exhibition matches in Saudi Arabia. When he finished, the king was so impressed with Palmer's expertise that he desired to give Palmer a gift. Palmer, a multimillionaire in his own right, demurred: "It isn't really necessary. I just enjoyed meeting your people and playing in your country."

The king indicated his extreme displeasure at not being able to give the golf pro a gift. Palmer wisely reconsidered and said, "Well, how about a golf club? A golf club would be a wonderful memento of my visit here." The king was pleased. The following day, a messenger delivered to Palmer's hotel room the title to a golf club, thirty-six holes, trees, lakes, buildings. The moral of this story? <u>In the presence of the king, don't ask for small gifts.</u>   *love this*

One day Jesus was walking down the road in Galilee and the blind man, Bartimaeus, called out, "Jesus, Son of David, have pity on me!" The apostles tried to hush him up. <u>But he cried louder,</u> "Jesus, Son of David, have pity on me!"

Jesus stops, turns, and asks, "What do you want?"

Without hesitation, the blind man says, "I want my sight!"

And Jesus says, "Your faith has saved you."

His sight was restored immediately and then Mark notes that Bartimaeus dropped his cloak. For a blind man, the cloak represented security, as the blind in first-century Palestine were considered cursed by God. Their families threw them in the streets. Their only protection against the elements was their cloak. He dropped his cloak. He dropped all the security he *all in* had ever known to follow the one named Jesus.

What do you want? Today, right now?

Boldly ask.

The one thing we owe absolutely to God
is never to be afraid of anything.
—Charles deFoucauld

CONSIDER THIS...

1. If Jesus were to ask you, right now—*what do you want?*—what would you say? Seriously, what would your answer be? *Happiness*

2. Bartimaeus had to drop his security blanket. What represents security for you? How is Jesus asking you to drop it? *Solitude, so find a community-effort!*

fire

Jesus Christ has irreparably changed the world.

When preached purely, His Word exalts, frightens, shocks, and forces us to reassess our whole life. The gospel breaks our train of thought, shatters our comfortable piety, and cracks open our capsule truths. The flashing spirit of Jesus Christ breaks new paths everywhere. His sentences stand like quivering swords of flame because He did not come to bring peace, but a revolution. The gospel is not a children's fairy tale, but rather a cutting-edge, rolling-thunder, convulsive earthquake in the world of the human spirit.

By entering human history, God has demolished all previous conceptions of who God is and what man is supposed to be. We are, suddenly, presented with a God who suffers crucifixion. This is not the God of the philosophers who speak with cool detachment about the Supreme Being. A Supreme Being would never allow spit on His face.

It is jarring indeed to learn that what He went through in His passion and death is meant for us too; that the invitation He extends is *Don't weep for Me! Join Me!* The life He has planned for Christians is a life much like He lived. He was not poor that we might be rich. He was not mocked that we might be honored. He was not laughed at so that we would be lauded. On the contrary, He revealed a picture meant to include you and me.

> IT MAKES ME HAPPY TO BE SUFFERING
> FOR YOU NOW, AND IN MY OWN BODY
> TO MAKE UP ALL THE HARDSHIPS THAT
> STILL HAVE TO BE UNDERGONE BY CHRIST
> FOR THE SAKE OF HIS BODY, THE CHURCH.
> (COL. 1:24 NJB)

By extinguishing the spirit that burns in the gospel, we scarcely feel the glow anymore. We have gotten so used to the ultimate Christian fact—Jesus naked, stripped, and crucified—that we no

What's our first response when things get hard?

longer see it for what it actually is. We are to strip ourselves of earthly cares and worldly wisdom, all desire for human praise, greediness for any kind of comfort, spiritual consolations included. The gospel is a summons to be stripped of those fine pretenses by which we manage to paint a portrait of ourselves for the admiration of friends.

We really aren't that bad. Are we?

Even the last rag we cling to—the self-flattery that suggests we are being humble when we disclaim any resemblance to Jesus Christ—even that rag has to go when we are face to face with the crucified Son of Man.

Because we approach the gospel with preconceived notions of what it should say rather than what it does say, the Word no longer falls like rain on the parched ground of our souls. It no longer sweeps like a wild storm into the corners of our comfortable piety. It no longer vibrates like sharp lightning in the dark recesses of our nonhistoric orthodoxy. The gospel becomes, in the words of Gertrude Stein,

> *... a pattering of pious platitudes spoken by*
> *a Jewish carpenter in the distant past.*

For example, the first beatitude—

BLESSED ARE THE POOR IN SPIRIT,
FOR THEIRS IS THE KINGDOM OF HEAVEN.
(MATT. 5:3 NASB)

—has so long been presented as a moralizing threat to detach ourselves from money, materiality, and all creature comforts, that we
no longer see it for the grand reversal it is. Jesus said, in effect,

BE LIKE A LITTLE CHILD. CONSIDER
YOURSELF TO BE OF LITTLE ACCOUNT.

BLESSED ARE YOU IF YOU LOVE TO BE
UNKNOWN AND REGARDED AS NOTHING.

To prefer contempt to honor, ridicule to praise, humiliation
to glory—these are some of the classic formulas of Christian
greatness.

Words like these not only call us to conversion, but they also
announce the Good News, that the messianic era has erupted
into history. For Christians living in what Oscar Cullman calls

"the isness of the shall be" they lay out the game plan for a radically different lifestyle of constant prayer, total unselfishness, buoyant, creative goodness, and unbridled involvement in God, His church, and the well-being of His children.

But let's be honest. Passages such as "This is the will of God, your holiness" (1 Thess. 4:3 NAB) cause apprehension, disquiet, and a vague sense of existential guilt. *Holiness* is a terrifying word when spoken by the living God. Living the paschal mystery, dying daily to self, and rising to newness of life in Christ is a fearful thing to contemplate, much less live.

Yet, there is something smoldering in His invitation— *Come, follow Me!*

We have all experienced the sadness of a Christian life that is secure, well regulated, but basically impoverished. We long, at least occasionally, for a generosity that would lift us above ourselves. Leon Bloy's words have the taste of truth:

The only true sadness is not to be a saint.

The resolution of this conflict is often initiated by what the late Dom Verner Moore called a "quasi-experiential realization of the warmth and tenderness of God's love." Or what

I choose to call "baptism by fire." This can happen in weekly worship, by hearing the Scripture, in shared prayer, even by holding an infant. It is available to anyone who steadfastly seeks to move beyond theoretical abstractions to living experience, intensely real. It proclaims further procrastination undesirable and precipitates the advent of the only adventure left to men and women, what Christopher Fry calls "the exploration into God."

in the moment, not to worry

It is natural to feel fear and insecurity when confronted with the radical demands of the Christian commitment. But enveloped in the lived truth of God's furious love, insecurity is swallowed up in the solidity of *agape*, and anguish and fear give way to hope and desire. The Christian becomes aware that God's appeal for unlimited generosity from His people has been preceded from His side by a limitless love, a love so intent upon a response that He has empowered us to respond through the gift of His own Spirit.

IN THIS IS LOVE, NOT THAT WE
LOVED GOD, BUT THAT HE LOVED US
AND SENT HIS SON TO BE THE
PROPITIATION FOR OUR SINS....

WE LOVE, BECAUSE HE FIRST LOVED US.
(1 JOHN 4:10,19 NASB)

Because of His furious love, you can burn.

A strange feeling comes over you,
when you see the silent candle burning.

If you recoil in fear, as Goethe concludes,

You are only a troubled guest
on the dark earth. [9]

1. Henri Nouwen said, "When the imitation of Christ
   does not mean to live a life like Christ, but to live
   your life as authentically as Christ lived his, then
   there are many ways and forms in which a man can
   be a Christian."[10] Sit with this quote a few minutes,
   asking the Father to speak to you through it.

   many chasing wrong thing

   own strengths

   meant to use them

2. Is the gospel alive and real to you right now? Or
   has it grown stale and predictable? Or is there some
   other way, possibly some both/and term you would
   use to describe it? *new light*

giving

Once or twice in a lifetime you hear a story that leaves an indelible mark on your heart and mind. Such is this story. I first heard it in 1967. It is Shel Silverstein's *The Giving Tree.*

"Once there was a tree ... and she loved a little boy." And so begins the story of a tree being happy because she is able to make the boy happy. At first the boy desires nothing but to climb on her branches, eat her apples, and lie in her shade.

But as the boy grows, so do his desires. But because of the tree's love, she gives her apples for him to sell for money to have real fun; her branches that he might build a house for a wife and family; and her trunk so he could build a boat and sail away from the boredom of life.

And then one day, the prodigal returns to the tree that loves him. By now, she has given him everything; all that remains of her is an old stump. The boy, now an old man, needs only a quiet place to sit and rest. And the Giving Tree gives once more.[11]

Ever since hearing that story many years ago, I've loved Silverstein's parable. It reminds me of Jesus, of whom Paul wrote in Philippians, "He emptied himself." He cried from His heart, nails in His hands, and poured out His blood that we might believe His love for us. Significantly, Jesus chose the giving tree, His cross, as the demonstrative sign of His absolutely furious love for men and women. In the words of one early church father: "the mightiest act of love ever to arise from a human soul."

How is it then that we've come to imagine that Christianity consists primarily in what we do for God? How has this come to be the good news of Jesus? Is the kingdom that He proclaimed to be nothing more than a community of men and women who go to church on Sunday, take an annual spiritual retreat, read their Bibles every now and then, vigorously oppose abortion, don't watch x-rated movies, never use vulgar language, smile a lot, hold doors open for people, root for the favorite team, and get along with everybody? Is that why Jesus went through the bleak and bloody horror of Calvary? Is that why He emerged in shattering glory from the tomb? Is that why He poured out His Holy Spirit on the church? To make nicer men and women with better morals? *no — not the calling → create! love!*

The gospel is absurd and the life of Jesus is meaningless unless we believe that He lived, died, and rose again with but one purpose in mind: to make brand-new creations. Not to make people with better morals, but to create a community of prophets and professional lovers, men and women who would surrender to the mystery of the fire of the Spirit that burns within, who would live in ever greater fidelity to the omnipresent Word of God, who would enter into the center of it all, the very heart and mystery of Christ, into the center of the flame that consumes, purifies, and sets everything aglow with peace, joy, boldness, and extravagant, furious love. This, my friends, is what it really means to be a Christian. Our religion never begins with what we do for God. It always starts with what God has done for us, the great and wondrous things that God dreamed of and achieved for us in Christ Jesus.

made he
path

1. Some have considered Silverstein's parable to be a story of selfishness and greed by the boy and irresponsible passivity by the tree. What do you think? *Puff the magic dragon } always return to it parents love*

2. As Timothy Jackson, a professor of Religious Studies at Stanford University put it: "Is this a sad tale? Well, it is sad in the same way that life is sad. We are all needy, and, if we are lucky and any good, we grow old using others and getting used up. Tears fall in our lives like leaves from a tree. Our finitude is not something to be regretted or despised, however; it is what makes giving (and receiving) possible.... Should the tree's giving be contingent on the boy's gratitude? If it were, if fathers and mothers waited on reciprocity before caring for their young, then we would all be doomed."[12] *give without fear & expectations...*

unimaginable
love

Perhaps the gut issue is not how much theology we have studied or how much Scripture we have memorized. All that really matters is this: *Have you experienced the furious longing of God or not?* yes

This very question provoked the brilliant Karl Rahner to prophesy:

> *In the days ahead, you will either be a mystic* why that word?
> *(one who has experienced God for real)*
> *or nothing at all.*

In times of persecution, theoretical Christianity will collapse.

Contemplation of the furious longing of God is elevated to a dramatic level in those rare and unforgettable moments when our faith, hope, and love are raised to an unprecedented level by the Holy Spirit's active intervention, much like being in that boat as the storm hits. We are plunged into mystery, or what Heschel called *radical amazement.* Self-consciousness and self-awareness disappear. We are in the presence of the ineffable Mystery above all creatures and beyond all telling.

These are moments of truth. You are alone with The Alone. God's tender feelings for you are no longer dry knowledge. You experience a certainty of God's longing for intimacy unlike anything you've felt in hand-clapping worship or anointed Scripture studies. Too many of us have received knowledge without appreciation, facts without enthusiasm. Yet, when the scholarly investigations were over, we were struck by the insignificance of it all. It just didn't matter.

When the night is bad and my nerves are shattered and the waves break over the sides, Infinity speaks. God Almighty shares through His Son the depth of His feelings for me, His love flashes into my soul, and I am overtaken by mystery. These are moments of *kairos*—the decisive inbreak of God's fury into my personal life's story.

It is then I face a momentous decision. Shivering in the rags of my seventy-four years, I have two choices. I can escape below into skepticism and intellectualism, hanging on for dear life. Or, with radical amazement, I can stay on deck and boldly stand in surrendered faith to the truth of my belovedness, caught up in the reckless raging fury that they call the love of God. And learn to pray.

afterword

by Claudia Mair Burney

award-winning author of *Wounded*

www.RagamuffinDiva.blogspot.com

I'm Mair. I'm a ragamuffin.

I'm Mair. I'm a diva.

Both of these are true.

Once upon a time, I was more than broken; I was *destroyed*, shattered—I believed—beyond repair. When I went to church, which was rare, I couldn't hold my head up. If you'd have asked me what God called me, my answer wouldn't have been "His Beloved." I would have said He calls me "His biggest disappointment."

But then a fury blew a book into my hands—*The Ragamuffin Gospel.*

Brennan Manning came to me bearing good news. He told me I am God's ragamuffin, a poor and needy *least of these*, and God loves me, just as I am. At the same time—oh glorious paradox!—he told me that there was a spark of the divine in me. He made real the words of Genesis 1:26, "Let us make man in our own image, in the likeness of ourselves." And that, beloved, makes me a humble diva. I'm indebted to Brennan for the gift of revealing to me exactly who I am, *ragamuffin diva*.

And now, the fury roars again. *The Furious Longing of God* has fanned that spark of resident divinity into a blazing flame of burning love. I've been swept into the embrace of God, in all His fury. And this fury, this sublime, ineffable fury is not God's anger. Oh no, it's His inexhaustible, unreasonable, and downright insane love.

The Furious Longing of God is not just a stripped-down-to-the-naked-truth treatise on the crazy love of the divine Madman. It is veritable *creed* for ragamuffins—and who wouldn't want to be a ragamuffin after reading this? Brennan has given us in this work postmodern Beatitudes:

> *You are blessed! God's desire is for you. And*
> *Jesus is the incarnation of God's furious*
> *longing. He is your supreme Lover. It's true.*

You are blessed. Your soul's winter is over.
The snows are over and gone. Flowers
are blooming inside of you. The season
of joyful songs has come. To you.

You are blessed! The love of God is folly. No
one is excluded. All (really!) are called to
the banquet table. Come, and be filled.

You are blessed! Be-YOU-ti-full. Be
you. Just be. Love supports you.

You are blessed! You have learned
the purpose of life: LOVE.

You are blessed! You can pray like
a child, and enjoy God.

You are blessed! Heal, and be healed. Reclaim
affirmations for the kingdom of God.

Amen. Amen. Amen.

Go now, beloved brothers and sisters, aflame with what you know to do: *Love!* Do not keep silent. Do not keep quiet, until righteousness goes forth like brightness and salvation is a torch burning. Until all nations see your righteousness, and all kings your glory. You will be called, "The evidence of God's love in the world."

Invite all to God's feast of furious love. Do as the Master commands, "Go out at once into the streets and lanes of the city and bring in here the poor and crippled and blind and lame" (Luke 14:21 NASB).

Bring them starving. Bring them bleeding and broken. Drag them to the banquet, wretched and raggedy as they are. Sit them at the table, though they mourn and weep, necks bent and heads hung low.

Go in love. Go with love. Go because of love.

How else will they know our good God?

How else will we?

"By this all men will know that you are My disciples, if you have love for one another" (John 13:35 NASB).

—Claudia Mair Burney
December 1, 2008, first week of Advent.

endnotes

1   Rich Mullins, "The Love of God" from the album *Never Picture Perfect* (Reunion, 1989).

2   Jean Vanier, *Drawn into the Mystery of God through the Gospel of John* (Mahwah, NJ: Paulist Press, 2004), 296.

3   Gerald May as quoted in Thomas L. Brodie's, *The Gospel According to John* (New York: Oxford University Press).

4   *Dictionary of the Bible* (New York: Macmillian, 1965) 269.

5   Thomas L. Brodie, *The Gospel According to John* (New York: Oxford University Press), 60–61.

6   Antony Campbell, *God First Loved Us* (Mahwah, NJ: Paulist Press, 2001), 26.

7   Hans Urs Von Balthasar, *Heart of the World* (Fort Collins, CO: Ignatius Press, 1980).

8   Miguel De Cervantes, *Don Quixote* [Volume 1/Chapter XIII] (New York: Harper Perennial, 2005).

9   Johann Wolfgang von Goethe, "The Holy Longing."

10   Henri Nouwen, *The Wounded Healer* (New York City: Image, 1979) 99.

11 Shel Silverstein, *The Giving Tree* (New York: Harper Collins, 1964).

12 Timothy Jackson, "The Giving Tree: A Symposium" © *First Things* 49, 1995, 22–45.

Bible resources

about the author

Brennan Manning has spent the past forty years helping others experience the reality of God's love and grace. It's at the heart of everything he's written and done. A recovering alcoholic and former Franciscan priest, his spiritual journey has taken him down a variety of paths. He has taught seminarians, spoken to packed arenas, lived in a cave and labored with the poor in Spain, and ministered to shrimpers in Alabama. Brennan is best known as the author of the contemporary classics *The Ragamuffin Gospel*, *Abba's Child*, *Ruthless Trust*, and *The Importance of Being Foolish*.